Talking to my Heart

Talking to my Heart

DEVOTIONAL

BOB NOVAK

Copyright © 2006 by Bob Novak.

ISBN: Softcover   1-4257-1439-0

All rights reserved. No part of this book may be reproduced or transmitted in any form or by any means, electronic or mechanical, including photocopying, recording, or by any information storage and retrieval system, without permission in writing from the copyright owner.

Scripture taken from:

Scripture taken from the **HOLY BIBLE, NEW INTERNATIONAL VERSION**
Copyrights 1973,1978,1984 by International Bible Society. Used by permission of Zondervan Publish House.

AMG Publishers Copyright 2000
King James Version Holy Bible
Chattanooga, Tennesee

This book was printed in the United States of America.

To order additional copies of this book, contact:
Xlibris Corporation
1-888-795-4274
www.Xlibris.com
Orders@Xlibris.com

Contents

Renovation	9
Repentance	10
Prayer for your life	11
Looking toward heaven	12
Don't give up	13
Trusting God	14
Forgiveness	15
Success in the eyes of God	16
Living in adversity	17
Loving God	18
Petitioning the Lord	19
Resurrection	20
Miracles	21
Anger	22
Personal Persecution	23
Finding a home	24
Having a heart filled with thankfulness	25
Living in Drunkenness	26
Jealousy of others	27
God's Power	28
Prayers of faith	29
God's Provision and Love	30
Why do we judge others?	31
Meditating on the word	32
Trials	33
Rapture	34
The Son of God	35
Faithfulness	36
Trusting in the Lord	37
Golden Jerusalem	38
God's Commandments	39

Truth	40
Peace	41
Meekness	42
Being light	43
Loving God back	44
Preventing an argument	45
Good deeds unto others	46
Acceptance	47
Taking a step of Faith	48
Angels	49
Being sealed with the Holy Spirit	50
Depending on God and Other People	51
Treasure	52
Brokenness	53
Bringing up kids	54
Loosing out on opportunity	55
Changing your surroundings	56
Growing like a red oak	57
Not Growing Weary	58
God fills us with his Spirit	59
Experiencing God's Help	60
Encouragement	61
Love	62
Love	63
Spiritual Experience	64
Turning my eyes on God	65
Reputation	66
Giving to the needy	67
Jesus' Authority	68
Living beyond Death	69
Victory over death	70
Being a Faithful Husband	71
Armor of God	72
Being a Marathon Runner	73
Reflections	74
Caring about each Other	75
God supplies us with what we need	76
Nailing our sins to the Cross	77
Having a Problem	78

Good Deeds	79
One day at a time	80
Renovation	81
Repentance	82
Prospering in life	83
The happy ending	84
Heart's Desire	85
Turn your burden to God	86
Angel's care	87
God the Judge	88
Healing of the Nations	89
God's eternal Love	90
Meditating on the word	91
Trials	92
Rapture	93
The Son of God	94
Faithfulness	95
Gossip	96
Golden Jerusalem	97
God's Commandments	98
Abiding in the vine	99
Bearing fruit	100
Pruning us back	101
You're invited	102
Gates of heaven	103
Instruction	104
Having no Fear because God is on your side	105
God is good	106
God works things for our good	107
Trusting in your self	108
Finding a home	109
Sin Vs. Sins	110
Jesus does Miracles	111
Jesus eats with the tax Collector	112
Jesus pays his tax	113
Trusting in the Lord	114
Crucifixation Prophecy	115
Drunkenness	116
Jesus betrayal	117

God's Power	118
Asking for a big thing	119
God's Provision and Love	120
Who should judge?	121
Meditating on the word	122
Trials	123
Rapture	124
The Son of God	125
Faithfulness	126
Trusting in the Lord	127
Golden Jerusalem	128

Renovation

Romans 8:28

For those God foreknew he also predestined to be conformed to the likeness of his Son—.

    When you renovate your house or car, you change the appearance of the house or car. When God renovates your heart your life shows His love. Also, your life reflects Jesus. Sometimes the change is painful to under go, and it hurts when your in it. But God's renovation is all for God's will.

    Whatever the things are that God chooses to do in your life, it molds you to the likeness of his Son Jesus. Being like Jesus you will show fruits of the Spirit.

    Transformation will be a life long process that will change the appearance of your life to others around you. If anyone asks you why you what happened to you tell them that you now have a personal relationship with Jesus.

Repentance

Luke 13:3

I tell you, no! but unless you repent you too will perish.

    Repentance is necessary to come to salvation. God wants everyone to come to repentance and come to salvation. If you tell him the sins you have committed before his eyes it is a promise that He will forgive you.

    Believers that are children of God will need to clean house if they are sinning. By confessing your wrongs you will have a right relation with God and able to do his will. It is also a promise that you will receive the Holy Spirit if you repent. If you are not a believer yet, repent and believe in Jesus and God will accept you as his children. Being a child of God you will go to heaven instead of perishing.

Prayer for your life

John 16:23

In that day you will no longer ask me anything. I tell you the truth, my Father will give you whatever you ask in my name.

Jesus told his disciples that they need to make their requests know to God. After Jesus rose from the dead, he ascended into heaven where he intercedes for us. When I have a need I make it know to God and I ask in Jesus name. When my prayers are answered I feel God cares and is working within my life. Talking to God is a valuable thing in my life.

Over the centuries, many miracles have been done in the name of Jesus. God cares about us very much. If you have faith in God, God can move mountains through your prayers.

Ask God for anything, no thing is too small or too big for God. If God answers your prayer you will feel like he cares about you.

Looking toward heaven

Colossians 3:2

Set your minds on things above, not on earthly things.

When I think about heaven my problems seem insignificant. This helps me cope with life. We are supposed to have joy in our problems and successes, but having joy always is sometimes hard to dig up.

Heaven is going to be paradise. So why do I forget about it, and get caught up in the worlds problems. If, I remember that Christ died for me so I could live with him forever my life seems worth living. Pulling your self out of depression is difficult, but remembering that Christ will raise my dead body back to life makes me have hope for the future.

Don't give up

Mark 14:34

"My soul is overwhelmed with sorrow to the point of death," he said to them. "Stay here and keep watch."

When Jesus said this he was facing death on a cross. Not a nice problem to endure, but he did. When I feel like giving up and I am filled with sorrow I remember what Jesus had to deal with.

He was filled with sorrow to the point of death. If you feel like this, remember that Jesus had victory over death and you will too because of him.

1 Corinthians 15:58 But Thanks be to God! He gives us the victory through our Lord Jesus Christ.

If you need help to get through your valley, ask someone who is capable of helping you. People need people and don't forget that people need God too.

Trusting God

Proverbs 3:7

Do not be wise in your own eyes;

Many times people ask me what are you going to do? Without thinking I say something. My mind is always on self propulsion. I need to take a step back and let God run my life. Turning my will over to God helps get everything back in step.

My thoughts are sometimes not always the best thing for me. When I think of something it may not be God's will or what he wants for me. So, simple trust in God has a way of letting things turn out for the best. If, I trust in myself disaster my occur in my life. When everything is going the way is supposed to, life is peaceful.

Forgiveness

Ephesians 4:32

Be kind and compassionate to one another, forgiving each other, just as in Christ God forgave you.

Traffic can be a thing that aggravates everyone. An accident can be even worse. When someone is cutting me off, I get angry. The thing I need to do is forgive the person who upset me. This is not always an easy task.

God has forgiven us our sins and we need to forgive those who sin against us. Why hold on to resentment and have anger in your heart? The anger levels one can go to can make us sin even worse. After, we forgive someone our peace returns.

Forgiving each other sometimes is hard because is evolves releasing hurt feelings. The Our Father prayer is good to memorize because it focuses on both of these aspects.

Success in the eyes of God

Psalm 1:1

Blessed is the man who does not walk in the
counsel of the wicked or
stand in the way of sinners or
sit in the seat of mockers.

God loves you just the way you are. If you don't have a lot of money or a high position job, you are still loved by God. Maturity is something that comes from right living. If someone says you're immature, remember that even a 50 year old can act childish. Maturity isn't marked by your success. How we treat and love others is the real sign of maturity.

Being responsible is a character attribute that is necessary for life. The world wants you to follow its ways not in the Lord. This verse shows that one will succeed if they follow a righteous life.

Living in adversity

Corinthians 11:24-25

Five times I received from the Jews the forty lashes minus one. Three times I was beaten with rods, once I was stoned, three times I was ship wrecked, I spent a night and a day in the open sea,

If you are suffering from physical pain, look to the sufferings of Paul or that of the cross of Jesus. This was severe pain. Your pain may be in mental suffering. When we are in these states we may feel abandoned from God and others. So hold on to this verse Romans 8:38-39

For I am convinced that neither death nor life, neither the present nor the future, nor any powers, neither height nor depth, nor anything else in all creation, will be able to separate us from the love of God that is in Christ Jesus our Lord.

God loves us and everything here on earth is temporary. There is a season for pain, and there is a season for joy.

Loving God

Matthew 22:37-39

Jesus replied: "'Love the Lord your God with all your heart and with all your soul and with all your mind.'"

It's easy to love God when everything is good or going your way, but to love him in hurt is hard. I come to God more though when I feel great rather than when I'm in pain. Sometimes I feel like he forgets about me. This is when I need to read His Word and listen to his promises

He responds to my heart with His Word and heals my soul and mind.

John writes that we are to love our brothers before we can show love to God, also you can love God by obeying his commands. When I think of Jesus as a person in heaven or of God as a person in heaven my love can go out to them as a person that really loves me back.

Petitioning the Lord

Matthew 7:8

For everyone who asks receives; he who seeks finds; and to him who knocks, the door will be opened.

Sometimes I forget to get God involved with what I'm doing. Maybe, I think he doesn't care or just that I'm not that important to him. But this verse in Matthew shows that your request will be answered. Not like the phone answering machines of today that put you through a series of options and then on hold for a long time. God listens to our prayers the moment we talk to him. There is no busy signal with God and he won't put you on hold. The next time sometime little or big comes up pray to God, and understand that God wants to be involved with your life

Resurrection

1 Corinthians 6:14

By his power God raised the Lord from the dead, and will raise us also.

God loves us enough to die for us, and since God raised him from the dead he will raise us up with him. I like how this verse is read in the King James Bible. The verse reads that our dead bodies will be brought back to life.

Holding and meditating on a verse can give encouragement and strengthen ones weary soul.

I don't know what heaven is going to be like, but it is referred to as beautiful and paradise. I need to fix my thoughts on above and remember I am here on only a temporary visit.

Miracles

Psalm 78:13

He divided the sea and led them through;
He made the water stand firm like a wall.

When God brought the Jews out of the land of Egypt, His servant Moses watched the sea divide in two so that they could escape the encroaching army. This miracle gave the Jewish people hope for their future in the Promised Land. This must have been such an experience to have gone through. To see this amount of God's power at work right in front of their eyes must have increased their faith. That God exists and he is at work within their lives. They must have felt love and protection. When the Egyptians tried to follow they were drowned by the water, because the walls of water collapsed in on them. When God is with you no one stands a chance against you.

Anger

James 1:20

For man's anger does not bring about the righteous life that God desires.

    When people get angry at things and people, we lose our cool. Then we become filled with thoughts of revenge or retaliation. This leads us to act unlike the way God desires. We say all kinds of evil and might even do something bad.

    Ridding oneself of anger can be done by praising God with an attitude of gratitude. At first you may not feel like your praise matters but watch how it changes the state of your heart. God desires for us to be holy and live righteous lives and when you are angry it gives way to more sin. This verse shows that God abhors the continuous attitude of anger. Repent your sin of anger, and fix your relationship with God and others.

Personal Persecution

Mathew 5:11

Blessed are you when people insult you, persecute you and falsely say all kinds of evil against you because of me.

One day I was telling a friend about Jesus and someone I know walked bye. When he heard me mention the name of Jesus to my friend, he said an insulting remark to me and my friend. Not knowing what to do I said something back. My silence would have been golden. My witness to this friend may have been ruined. I actually cared about both of them, but I didn't respond to the situation properly.

I sure didn't feel or think I was blessed at the moment of the insult, but holding on to the word of truth of Mathew 5:11-12 I was. Being rejected by others is difficult when you are telling others the Gospel.

Finding a home

John 14:23

Jesus replied, "If anyone loves me, he will obey my teaching. My father will love him, and we will come to him and make our home with him.

    Jesus says that we will live with him if we obey his teaching. Spending life after death must be amazing, because we will be in heaven. Just think that after you die there's another home waiting for you on the other side. This is where you will spend eternity. Jesus paid the price for eternal life on the cross. No matter how many good things you do that's not enough to pay the price. He died for the wrongs you have done in the eyes of God. By believing in him and trusting him as savior all your sin will be covered by his blood.

Having a heart filled with thankfulness

Psalm 150:2

Praise him for his acts power;
Praise him for his surpassing greatness.

    Praising the lord is always good to do. God deserves our praise because he supplies us with everything which we need to live. We can praise him for taking care of us.

    We can praise the Lord because he died for us on a cross and gave his life as a ransom for all. He has granted to those who believe in him eternal life.

    We can praise the Lord when he answers big prayers in our lives. Things that seem impossible to us are possible for God to do. Sometimes we may not even realize God's at work within our lives. His greatness can be seen in the world he has made and with the love he sends to his children.

Living in Drunkenness

Ephesians 5:18

Do not get drunk on wine, which leads to debauchery. Instead be filled with the Spirit.

If you like to get drunk, you're sinning against God. Here in Ephesians we are told to put away with drunkenness and instead be filled with the Spirit.

The sin of drunkenness is one that after you're in it, it's hard to get out of. Like it is written sin gives birth to sin and when sin is full grown it brings death. Many of my friends in life have died due to this sin. The whole life style is one of rebellion against God. People trapped into this sin focus on the effects of bottle and worship it. Therefore they block out the Spirit and become useless to themselves and others.

Though, I know many, who have recovered from this sin. Ask God to forgive you and choose life instead of the drink.

Jealousy of others

John 11:57

But the chief priests and Pharisees had given orders that if anyone found out where Jesus was, he should report it so that they might arrest him.

    Just like the way the priests and Pharisees were jealous of Jesus, we too are sometimes jealous of others. I know some people who are just like the Pharisees and think of murdering the one they are jealous of. For Jesus it was his mission, he was to be betrayed into the hands of evil men and be crucified. This great injustice God turned into the greatest triumph of all time. Also, God made good out of evil, which is called divine providence.

    When we hold an evil thought or covet something another person has we are jealous. This jealousy could cause harm to ourselves and is a sin that God doesn't approve of. Live holy lives and be content with little.

God's Power

John 11:25 KJV

Jesus said unto her, I am the resurrection, and the life; he that believeth in me, though he were dead, yet shall he live:

When I think that God has the power to raise our bodies from the dead, I'm amazed. This is something I can't do and neither can you. This power rests only in God. Jesus is the resurrection and the life with this being he holds the keys to life and death.

There's a movie out Bruce Almighty and the actor has the power of God. God's power even in this comedy can be seen as dramatic and awesome. I guess people would like to have power over different things in life, but only God does. God can make something happen, if he chooses to let it occur.

But if you believe in Jesus, he says you will live after death.

Prayers of faith

Mark 22-23 KJV

And Jesus answering saith unto them, Have Faith in God. For Verily I say unto you, That whosoever shall say unto this mountain, Be thou removed, and be thou cast into the sea; and shall not doubt in his heart, but shall believe that those things which he saith come to pass; he shall have whatsoever he saith.

    Wow just think, God could answer a big prayer like that, but Jesus says you need to believe in your heart that it has already come to pass. Having faith in God to move your mountain what ever it be, could be difficult because sometimes we forget what God is capable of.

    Plus, if God has just done something great in your life you may have more faith than before. Psalm 78 tells about Moses' answered prayers. Read about prayers answered by God in the Holy Bible.

God's Provision and Love

Romans 5:8 KJV

But God commendeth his love toward us, in that while we were yet sinners, Christ died for us.

Jesus choosing to give his life for me is amazing. Jesus loves me enough to die for me. Jesus' mission was the cross. His cross and his shed blood on it wipes away all my sin. Every time I worry about my sin I just have to bring it to the cross and remember Jesus death was its payment. God accepts his sacrifice for the sins of the whole world.

Everyone needs to come to repentance for eternal life. God's love provided a way and that is through his Son, Jesus. Jesus loves us enough to endure a cross of death. Think of all the pain and heart ache that was taken for us to be accepted as children of God.

Why do we judge others?

Luke 6:37

Do not judge and you will not be judged.

Many times, the way someone talks or dresses make us take an opinion of them. Possible we judge them and want to feel superior to them.

Maybe, we base our judgment on the fact that they are not saved and that judgment is for God alone. We should not play God or judge others because we ourselves are not in right in doing so.

I have judged others not knowing the evil that was stored up in my heart. You only need to worry about your own sin and repent from it, and do not worry about someone else's sin and judge them because of it.

Meditating on the word

Matthew 4:4

Jesus answered "It is written: Man does not live on bread alone but on every word that comes from the mouth of God."

Being a child of God you will need to meditate on word of God and live on it. It will show you God's will and his law. This will encourage, strengthen, and give you hope. It will encourage you to live a holy life. It will strengthen your faith. It will give hope for the future.

How can you obey the law without knowing it? Keeping your mind fresh in his commands makes you walk a righteous life.

When you walk in the path of righteousness, it is by the Holy Spirit who dwells within you.

Trials

James 1:12

Blessed is the man who perseveres under trial, because when he has stood the test, he will receive the crown of life that God has promised to those who love him.

I once had a problem with the heat in my apartment and I thought it would never be right. This was a trial that I didn't take with grace. I was so angry that I almost became of no use to myself. This problem was frustrating enough to make me yell at the ones I love.

My confidence in God to solve this problem was small. This just seemed to aggravate me.

The man who perseveres under trail will build his faith strong, and upon it will save his soul. We face many trails in life and there's always another one around the bend. So we need to have thee endurance of a marathon runner.

Rapture

Corinthians 15:51-52

Listen, I tell you a mystery: We will not all sleep, but we will all be changed—
In a flash, in the twinkling of an eye, at the last trumpet. For the trumpet will sound, the dead will be raised imperishable, and we will be changed.

    The prophecy of the rapture some day will be fulfilled. At this time, believers will meet Christ in the air and have a new spiritual body and live with Christ forever. Those that have died will be there too, and they will receive a new body also. This event could happen at any time because Jesus said I am coming soon.
    So we should walk obedient and holy lives. That would make the Lord happy. Just think you may meet the Lord in the air any day now. This can give you strength to get through the day. If you are in pain or suffering, hold on because Jesus is coming for you.

The Son of God

Romans 1:4

And who through the Spirit of holiness was declared with power to be the Son of God by his resurrection from the dead: Jesus Christ our Lord.

Jesus was in heaven before he came to earth. Jesus was born into this world though the virgin Mary and conceived by the Holy Spirit. Jesus existed since the beginning of time and now sits at the right hand of the Father.

When Jesus asked Peter who he thought he was, Peter answered, Matthew 16:16 "you are the Christ, the Son of the living God." Jesus said he had authority to lay down his body and authority take it up from the dead. Jesus said he would destroy the temple and would raise it up in three days, and Jesus did so. His resurrection from the dead shows the Power of God and establishes that he is the Son of God.

Faithfulness

Proverbs 3:3

Let love and faithfulness never leave you; bind them around your neck, write them on the tablet of your heart.

In the Book of Proverbs this chapter says you will win favor in the sight of God and Man if you never let love and faithfulness leave you. I found this to be true. People respect it when you say you are going to be some where and you are. If you are not some where you are supposed to be people lose trust in you. I like to try to keep all my appointments.

Also I try to love my friends, God, and family as much as I can. The sinful nature breaks my relationships apart and causes a disconnection of love. God's favor will be given to those who love him through obedience and they will be blessed. The same is somewhat true about your friends if they are genuine.

Trusting in the Lord

Proverbs 3:5

Trust in the Lord with all your heart
And lean not on your own understanding;

    When I trust in the lord I have peace. When I trust in myself I have negative projection and worry. Though in life it is necessary to take action when you have a problem, I find letting God care about it gives me peace. Prayer helps turn it over into the hands of God.

    People ask me "What am I going to do about it?" The next thing that happens is I lean on my own understanding instead of trusting that God will work it out for me. I could worry forever, but that wouldn't achieve anything good.

    God solved the problem of salvation and if you trust in him he will bring you home to heaven. If you trust in him you will never be put to shame.

Golden Jerusalem

Revelation 21:18

The wall was made of pure jasper, and the city of pure gold, as pure as glass.

　　God has made the city beautiful as a bride dressed for her husband. Our new heavenly home will be built by God and not by us. People build our homes here on earth. Why is God building us a city? I think it is because we will need a place to live and to worship the Lord. Possible the city will have rooms for the rewards a believer gets upon his or her judgment of works.

　　We are not saved by works but we will receive rewards for our actions here on earth. Are souls are saved by our faith in Jesus. We are not under the wrath of God if we believe in Jesus.

God's Commandments

Psalm 119:59

I have considered my ways and have turned my steps to your statutes.

    When God's commandments are broken by me, I have to be forgiven by God and not by me. God forgives them after I confess them to him. So the commandments are Gods and they need to be forgiven by God.

    After I repent of my sin, the guilt I have will lift and my heart will be in right before God Almighty. When I turn to Gods statutes I can live a righteous life and be blessed by God with blessings that unfold into my life everyday.

Truth

John 14:6

Jesus saith unto him, I am the way, the truth, and the life; no man cometh unto the Father, but by me.

The truth in the world is a relative sort of thing. Each one believes that something is right in there own eyes and that is the truth. But Jesus said that he is the truth in the eyes of God. When people tell you theirs another way to heaven other than Jesus don't believe it. This verse says that there is no other way to God but by the way of Jesus.

Speaking the truth is not always easy when we are put in a sticky situation. God forgives us when we confess to telling lies.

The Holy Bible is the truth, and it was defined as truth in the American, dictionary in 1873.

Peace

John 14:27

Peace I leave you, my peace I give unto you; not as the world giveth, give I unto you. Let not your heart be troubled, neither let it be afraid.

    I have peace when I let God take of my problems and worries. If I worry about stuff my heart is troubled and I become afraid of the future. If I have peace in the midst of all my tribulations, my life is calm like when the breeze stops after a storm. When the disciples where in the midst of a storm, Jesus commanded the sea and wind to calm down. The storm died down and the disciples felt peace. This peace is available to us through Jesus. Let Jesus calm your storms and give you peace and serenity.

    When my peace is at hand, I can face hardship even though it is painful and difficult. So don't give up in the face of temptation, and you will win the crown of life.

Meekness

Matthew 5:5

Blessed are the meek, for they will inherit the earth.

The word meek actually means controlled by the Spirit of God. When we are controlled by the Spirit, we respond to situations the way God would want us to. For example taming ones anger would show that you are now meek instead of hot headed.

The Lord Jesus described himself as meek. We should follow his example. Sometimes it is best to take a lower seat instead of one of prominence and another way is to humbly accept compliments.

Jesus has said that the meek will inherit the earth and this is Promise of God. So, remember that the next time you feel like lifting yourself up let someone else do it to you.

Being light

Matthew 5:16

Let your light shine before men, that they may see your good works, and glorify your Father which is in heaven.

One day I was riding the school bus home from school, and this girl asked me why don't you make fun of people and bust their chops back. She said that she saw something different in me than in her other friends. When I answered her back I should have said it was because of Christ but I didn't. I said I don't like that kind of joking around. If someone's light is shining their deeds before men or women will be thought of as acceptable and honorable. To this girl it must have been a surprise to her when I didn't say mean things to the other kids on the bus. Looking back now I can see that being nice to others attracted her to a relationship with Jesus Christ, though I don't know if she ever became a believer in Christ.

Loving God back

John 14:15

If ye love me, keep my commandments.

To love God back, I need to be obedient to his commands. This is very difficult when the world pushes us around everyday. We need to stand with the Word of God in our hearts and practice what it says. Sometimes I slip up and sin and I don't do what I read. So I have to confess to my wrongs, then I able to walk a life that Christ would want.

With temptation all over the media it's hard not to follow their ways. But remember that love for the world is enemies with God. We don't need to separate ourselves from the world but instead we need to let the Holy Spirit transform us so that we maintain our position with godly living.

Preventing an argument

Proverbs 17:14

Starting a quarrel is like breaching a dam; So drop the matter before a dispute breaks out.

When someone starts a fight, the matter is brought upon by the tongue. If you are wise you will drop the matter before you get into a heated fight.

This happens to my mom and I very often and I don't like it. I would to drop the conversation but I don't and neither does she. I like when there is peace in my family but many times we argue and fight. I guess the whole matter could be averted if I dropped the matter completely. Try this the next time you feel like the dam is going to break down on you.

Good deeds unto others

James 2:26

As the body without the spirit is dead, so faith without deeds is dead.

When we die our spirit leaves our body, but while we live we should show our faith by doing good deeds. Doing good deeds comes naturally to me except when I am angry. Then it is hard to think of others. I am surprised when my Christian friends do something good for me. I feel like I don't desire a nice deed once in a while. This is probably because of the world we live in. The world we live in will strip your mind of the righteous life that can be found in Christ.

This life will be found in heaven as well and with more abundance. The next time someone asks for help or a favor think that by helping them out you will serve God. When God sees the good you do he will reward you for such actions.

Acceptance

Luke 22:42

Father if you are willing, take this cup from me; yet not my will, but yours be done.

Jesus must have been suffering so badly at the thought of his death. So, he asked his Father for an alternative plan. After, he realized this is what God wanted he had to accept the death of a criminal. This much acceptance is incredible. His death would be the payment for all of sins of the world. God choose that his blood on the cross would justify us.

The problems people face are troubling because we don't accept any outcome except the outcome of our choice. To choose to let people and things be the way their going to be instead of what we wish is difficult. Remember that if Jesus could accept something so unfair we should be able to accept the things life chooses to throw at us.

Taking a step of Faith

Matthew 14:28-30

"Lord if it's you," Peter replied, "tell me to come to you on the water."
"Come," he said.
Then Peter got down out of the boat, walked on the water and came toward Jesus. But when he saw the wind, he was afraid and beginning to sink, cried out, "Lord save me!"

It's hard to take a step a faith like Peter but not impossible. If you want to experience the awesome power of God sometimes you have to step out of the boat. I am just saying this literally. I don't mean get out of boat you might be in. Taking a step of faith may seem illogical but will draw you closer to God himself. This is because if God responds to your prayer you will be surprised. Also, you may experience a sense of gratitude and closeness like never before.

Angels

Psalm 34:7

The angel of the Lord encamps around those who fear him, and he delivers them.

Who doesn't want God on their side when it comes to life? I sure do. This verse says that God's angel will be around you if you fear him. When I am in sin, I'm not in fear of the Lord. So, God possible lifts some of the protection he has on us.

I believe the angel of the Lord will protect us from harmful things. I wish I could remember this. It would give such a feeling of protection. The Lord should be at the center of my focus though. As this verse says that the angel of the Lord encamps around those who fear him, this should build you up in your courage. Because the Lord is going to protect you with one of His angels.

Being sealed with the Holy Spirit

Ephesians 1:13

And you also were included in Christ when you heard the word of truth, the gospel of your salvation. Having believed, you were marked in him with a seal, the promised Holy Spirit,

When I first heard the word of salvation, I was filled with hope for heaven. I believe this was threw the Holy Spirit.

Romans 15:13

This verse in Ephesians tells us that the moment we believe in Christ for salvation, the Holy Spirit is put into us. We don't need to anything to get it. No other point other than that moment you first believed to acquire the Holy Spirit is necessary. Don't be mislead that you need to do anything else. The people in the Bible acquired it the same way.

Depending on God and Other People

Ecclesiastes

4:9   Two are better than one—

4:12— And a three cord is not quickly broken

God shows that a wife and husband have unity and strength together. Also God shows that a rope or cord is not easily broken if is united with three strands. The three strands represent you, God, and a friend. Also, the three cord Strands could represent you and your wife and God. When they are brought together the strength is strong. If a couple is broken their strength is diminished apart. Likewise if a person loses his unity with God and others is torn apart their strength to survive is destroyed. Since God, most of all helps us, we lose out on blessings when we try to do things independently. Keep in touch with God and others and you will have blessings and assistance of God and others.

Treasure

Luke 12:34

For where your treasure is, there your heart will be also.

Thinking of heaven should be your first priority. When we think that our treasure is in our bank accounts, we lose hold of what is really important. Jesus says we should set our hearts on the kingdom of the God instead of this world. This world will pass away but the one to come will last forever.

A treasure is commonly thought of as a treasure map and it's hid in the dirt where X marks the spot. But this is from people who were obsessed with the love of money. Try to redirect your heart on the real treasure and that is doing God's will. God's will is to preach the gospel, and save the sinners soul from the fire of hell.

Brokenness

Acts 9:9

For three days he was blind, and did not eat or drink anything.

Saul became Paul and when he was converted. This was done through brokenness. The Lord revealed himself to him and spoke with him. Paul fell to the ground and Jesus said to him why do you persecute me? As he was still know as Saul, he said Lord what must I do?

The brokenness process for Paul was sudden and then followed by a gradual process of years of trials. Each person that undergoes brokenness is only effective for the Lord when he is broken. Only then does Christ shine out of him instead of the old self. When you're broken you will focus on what God wants first and second on what the world wants.

After his brokenness, Paul became a great missionary for Christ in proclaiming the gospel.

Bringing up kids

Proverbs 19:18

Discipline your son, for in that there is hope; Do not be a willing party to his death.

Kids sometimes go down the wrong path due to peer pressure. When they due, they can get caught up in smoking, taking drugs, and drinking alcohol. This path could definitely kill them. An important thing to do is to punish them and send them to rehab. This will help them get on the right path.

If they start hanging out with the kids that got them in trouble, they will return to the reckless, abandon life style. It may hurt them to separate them form their so called friends, but this in the end, you will save their life. So discipline is necessary for putting your kids on the straight path.

Loosing out on opportunity

Psalm 25:2

In you I trust my God.
Do not let me be put to shame,
Nor let my enemies triumph over me.

    I don't like looking a loser. I know that God loves me just the way I am. Sometimes things don't work out the way they are planned. When this happens, I feel like giving up. They say that what doesn't kill you makes you harder. Disappointment is going to follow me around until I take action.

    David in this Psalm cries out to God for help and not to be hurt but be protected. Why does David ask for this? I believe it is to protect his life and not to lose anything he's endured to get. God says ten thousand will fall at your right side and twenty thousand at your left and you will stand in the midst protected. God provision for eternal life gives us victory at the end of our life if we are beset by adversity.

Changing your surroundings

Psalm 78:14

He guided them with the cloud by day and with light from the fire all night.

    If you move some where, God is still with you even though you may forget about him being in your life. God said he would never forsake you or leave you.
I forget about him, but he never forgets about us. Giving God some attention is a valuable commodity.

    I have moved around a lot in the last ten years and have had different homes. God is with me in each new house. Also, He is with me at work, at school if your in school, at the store, and outside in the car.

    I can pray where ever I am because God is always present and will never leave me. When my surroundings change it doesn't change the fact the God is with me.

Growing like a red oak

Psalm 1:3

He is like a tree planted by streams of water, which yields its fruit in season and whose leaf does not wither.
Whatever he does prospers.

Have you ever seen how good a tree grows that is planted by a stream of water? It grows up big and strong and full of leaves. I saw a tree by a river that must have been two hundred years old. Its trunk must have been five feet wide in diameter.

Trees are like people and people can grow and prosper if they follow a life planted in God. God will give you success if your ways are righteous. Following a righteous life can be difficult because people and the world will want you to follow its ways instead of the ways your conscience tells you to go. Plant yourself in God's Word and grow like a great red oak.

Not Growing Weary

Isaiah 40:31

Those who hope in the Lord will renew their strength.

When people lose their ability to go on with life, it is sometimes caused by taking their attention off of God. When you hope in the Lord, strength flows in your heart and mind. This gives you the endurance for life in the world we live. The type of strength that I have felt has been courage to under go the hardest of situations. Here's one for example.

When all the textile work shifted to out of the country, I was faced with little money. I worried that I would have enough to pay the bills. Then my mom got sick and my dad was facing a retirement that would be of low income. My truck broke down too. So, I hoped in the Lord and he gave me strength to face these problems and the good thing is that they all worked themselves out.

God fills us with his Spirit

Luke 17:21

The Kingdom of God is within you.

Our bodies are filled with the Holy Spirit and God lives within us. We should walk a life that would please God.

I once wondered, why do I like to help people. I thought at first that it was because I was a good person. But God revealed to me that it was his spirit living inside on me. God's spirit helps me love others around me. Naturally, I would tell people to do it themselves or get help from someone else. But, I choose to let my spirit come out and help them in spite of my own feelings. God likes this and the people I help like it too.

Experiencing God's Help

2 Timothy 4:17

The Lord stood at my side and gave me strength.

My appendix did not burst when I was infected, and I did not die when I was under the strong anesthesia. The Lord stood by me and helped me keep it together under all the circumstances. I cried when they told me all that could possibly happen to me. But I remembered that if I where to die, I would go and live with the Lord.

This hope for the future was the real thing that made me stay alive. I was only twelve then, but I can still remember that horrible night in the hospital. Everyone that loved me told me I would be okay. But they didn't know for sure what the outcome would be for me. When I came out of the anesthesia, I was in a lot pain. I recovered quickly thanks to the Lord's will. God had kept me alive to live another day.

Encouragement

1 Thessalonians 5:11

Encourage one another and build each other up.

    I was in wrestling during high school and I went to a private practice club. There I was encouraged to do the best I knew how. It was a lot of work and sweat. I worked at wrestling real hard until I broke my foot. The encouragement kept me focused on my goal.

    When you build someone up it can be done in a manner that you would like to be done unto you. People who go without any encouragement will feel like they are forgotten. This can cause depression. I know I like to be told I did something good or right. Sometimes people will give up if they are not encouraged. Tell someone a line of scripture and see them forget their problem.

Love

1 Corinthians 13:4

Love is patient, love is kind. It does not envy, it does not boast, it is not proud.

When someone does something nice for me I am surprised. Why is it? It is because I am not used to people who show the love of Christ. Sometimes I think they are up to something, but they are not. They are just showing me the love that God gives us.

I don't find that many people here in New Jersey are kind. At church possibly but out in the world, people are first come first serve basis. God allows this to happen. Even though, he wants his children to be loving and giving and not to act as the world is. Everyone at times finds themselves being unkind. Try to love people who need it the most.

Love

1 Corinthians 13:5

Love is not rude, it is not easily angered, it keeps no record of wrongs.

When I show the love of Christ, I will not remember the wrongs others have done to me. I will keep no record of wrongs, and forgive them.

Peter disowned Jesus Christ on the night of his betrayal, but Jesus forgave him and made him leader of the new Christian church.

People can do the same. They can forgive others who have wronged them. For myself I have problems with this. I hold on to hurt feelings way too long. I replay it in my mind and stay upset. If I show the love of Christ, I forgive because God has forgiven us. This should motivate us to forgive others.

Spiritual Experience

Matthew 17:2

There he was transfigured before them. His face shone like the sun, and his clothes became as white as the light.

The transfiguration of Jesus must have been an exciting for James, John, and Peter. They were experiencing a moment that they would never forget. Jesus was seen in a different radiance before them. The disciples were brought into a closer relationship with Jesus and knew something about him that would imprint them on their mind.

God gives us individual spiritual experiences. They come in all different ways and forms. People may see an angel, or people may have a great big prayer answered. People may have a dream, or people may have a healing. Whatever your experience is, God wants draw you closer.

Turning my eyes on God

Psalm 119:36

Turn my heart toward your statutes and not toward selfish gain.

If I look at all things I could possibly have or get, I forget about God. He is the giver of all such things and when I forget about God I'm in trouble. The gifts I get come from him and are not of my own making, although it can appear that way.

Looking at God's statutes and following them will make me a blessed person. Honoring God will create success. When I am greedy my end will be destruction because I will follow after evil in order to achieve selfish gain. Follow God and he will give you the desires of your heart

Reputation

Proverbs 22:1

A good name is more desirable than great riches; to be esteemed is better than silver or gold.

To attain a good reputation one must be faithful and honest. Desiring a good name is something that people seek after. If you're dishonest your reputation goes down. Also, if you are a drunk or get into a relationship with someone other than your spouse your status of standing in the community could drop. The media looks for things like this to happen to people in positions of power.

When you do something not approved of by either God or man, people look down on you. People are extremely quick to judge others. God tells us not to judge others because Jesus is the Judge of the living and the dead.

A person with a good reputation will feel good about one self.

Giving to the needy

Matthew 6:3

But when you give to the needy, do not let your left hand know what your right hand is doing.

Jesus tells us in this passage it is favorable to let your giving to the needy be done in secret. Feeding the poor, clothing the homeless, or sheltering someone are all things which help people. God likes when we help each other especially when people can't pay you back for your help.

I have been around people who have told me that I shouldn't give a poor, homeless person money because they will use it for alcohol. If no one reaches out with help what will these people do? They may spend it on alcohol and drugs, but you don't know what God could make happen for that person if you help them. In Luke he writes that the kingdom of God is for the poor.

Jesus' Authority

John 10:18

No one takes it from me, but I lay it down of my own accord. I have authority to lay it down and authority to take it up again. This command I received from my Father.

Jesus has control over life and death. This was granted to him from God the Father after his resurrection. He was an instrument from God that implored himself to save our souls from Satan's grasp. By his sacrifice our sins are forgotten.

People don't have this authority to bring back the dead or send someone to eternal glory. People are under the authority of governments and God foremost. You can have only one King. By surrendering oneself to God life has a wonderful way of working out bad situations.

Living beyond Death

John 11:25

Jesus said to her, "I am the resurrection and the life. He who believes in me will live, even though he dies."

    Jesus holds the power of life in his mouth. He can deliver us back to life after we have died. He holds the keys to life and death.

    By believing in Jesus, God will grant us life when we die. Living in great beyond will be spent with our friends and family in Christ and with Jesus, and his angels. Some people in the world think that they will be reincarnated or vanish like dust. Christians know they will live with God and live forever.

    Longing to live with Jesus is good. This is an encouraging attitude to have. It can transform a bad day into a day of rejoicing.

Victory over death

1 Corinthians 15:57

But thanks be to God! He gives us victory through our Lord Jesus Christ.

We don't have to work for our salvation. It is a gift from God. Jesus had victory and we will share eternal life because of it.

We will do good works to other out of our love for Jesus. He intends for us to do good works but not save us by our works. We are saved by his blood on the cross. If you have faith in Christ, you will show it by your good deeds. God's plan for salvation was sought for victory by Jesus on the cross. If, we could be as good as we wanted to be it still would never be enough for God. God sought that his Son would be the atonement, and not to let your being good the payment. We should through faith look to God not out of our own achievement.

Being a Faithful Husband

Ephesians 5:25

Husbands love your wives, just as Christ loved the church, and gave himself up for her.

When I saw the movie Brave heart, Mel Gibson, the actor showed the kind of self sacrifice one could give for their wife. In the movie, his wife is murdered, but his revenge is a love for her that is ever enduring. He takes on a whole army of the kings men to tell the king he's in charge. The movie is filled with tragedy and triumph. I don't think this would happen today, but it's a demonstration of the kind of love and sacrifice one could have for their wife.

Christ on the other hand demonstrated his love toward us by his sacrifice on the cross. To love your wife with that love is just too amazing. Love for your wife can be displayed by being faithful with no outside sexual relationships.

Armor of God

Ephesians 6:13

Therefore put on the full armor of God, so that when the day of evil comes, you may be able to stand your ground, and after you have done everything, to stand.

Sometimes it rains, sometimes it storms, and sometimes it is sunny. But don't be fooled your enemy the devil will attack your faith at some point in your life. When you're in the middle of a hurricane, your faith is tested to the limit. Believers are attacked. I heard that a missionary was killed by a tribe he was working with. His family extended love to the tribe that killed him and the tribal people felt remorse and became believers in Jesus Christ. For them this was their day of evil when their dad was killed. But instead of showing their hate they demonstrated love and the missionary's work of twenty years was finally becoming a victory.

Being a Marathon Runner

Philippians 3:14

I press on toward the goal to win the prize for which God has called me heavenward in Christ Jesus.

When a marathon runner competes in the Olympics and wins they get a medal for their achievement. Paul was like this. He had the stamina to finish the race of life. His Christian walk was a struggle and pressure. Although, we don't run the race, we walk. The pace is slow and is the length of our lives. It takes endurance to press on toward the goal when life seems overwhelming.

Paul faced being beaten with rods, ship wrecked, and stoned. His race was over when God called him home. When we are in the middle of pain it seems unpleasant but it brings forth righteousness. No one wants to face things like Paul. But because of it, he produced much of the New Testament.

Reflections

Proverbs 27:19

As water reflects a face,
So a man's heart reflects the man.

    When I look into a mirror or a reflection in a pool of water, I see myself. There have been times when I was displeased with my image, not because of what I looked like, but because of what I thought about myself. Having a good image can show that in the sight of God you are doing the right thing. If, you're not doing what God wills for you to do, you may look at your self in the mirror and feel like something is wrong with you.

    Your heart shows who you are by your actions and talk. When your heart is pure and not sinful you will do what God wills. Ask God for a heart that is willing to follow his commandments. Hopefully when you look in the mirror you will see a godly person.

Caring about each Other

Philippians 2:4

Each of you should look not only to your own interests, but to the interests of others.

If I show attention to my friend or parent, it shows them I care about them. Caring about other's interests gives others a sense of being accepted and important. Who doesn't like to have something done for them? Nobody. Everyone likes other people to show interest in the things they are doing. A genuine look, action, or word can lift another's spirit up when they are down.

Getting involved in another's business will get others to show you attention. If this doesn't happen remember that God cares about your interests and is working all your circumstances out for your good.

God supplies us with what we need

Philippians 4:19

And my God will meet all your needs according to his glorious riches in Christ Jesus.

I always have had enough food to eat. God made opportunities for work and food to be bought. When I hear people are starving, it's hard for me to believe it. It's true though some people don't have enough, but are they children of God? This promise above in scripture is for believers in Christ. Through out the years though, his people have had famines and droughts. Our society here in America has always had enough for the last couple of hundred of years. Thanksgiving was a holiday to commemorate this blessing from God. The next time you give thanks to God for your food remember he cares about you.

Nailing our sins to the Cross

Colossians 2:14

Having canceled the written code, with its regulations, that was against us and that stood opposed to us; he took it away, nailing it to the cross.

Jesus himself was nailed to the cross. He carried all our sin on that cross. Anything you did today or yesterday was taken away by that cross. It wasn't easy to bear that cross, so don't allow your sin to be taken lightly. His extreme love for us was shown by that cross.

God is not a liar, and he promises that your sin will be forgiven if you confess it to him. Remember that the cross and his blood on it wipes away our sin and transgressions. God is rich in mercy toward sinners who have repented. He prepared a way for us to come to him as a Father. The cross was thought of the worst possible punishment, but God turned it into a way of salvation for sinners.

Having a Problem

Proverbs 9:9

Instruct a wise man and he will be wiser still; teach a righteous man and he will add to his learning.

Having a problem today? If so I once heard it said, "If, you **think** you have **no problem** the problem doesn't *exist*." If I think about my problem, it stays in my mind. Forgetting about what bothers you can be done taking the attention off of yourself and thinking about others. When I help someone else I forget about what's bothering me. Forgetting about oneself can be a beautiful thing because not only are you helping someone else you're helping yourself. When all my problems are forgotten I feel much better.

Good Deeds

James 2:26

As the body without the spirit is dead, so faith without deeds is dead.

Faith can be shown through our deeds. Where there is faith you see someone who does good deeds because their love for God is made apparent. I can't always do good deeds because sometimes I am in the sinful nature. When this happens I am self centered and self absorbed. If I am in the spirit, I am a good servant for God and my actions show it.

When we show no good deeds our faith is invisible. Though we may be saved our life needs to be overhauled. Becoming a servant for Christ is not exactly what I think about everyday. I usually think about how I can pay the bills. If I have good deeds my faith is alive and living, whereas if I have no good deeds my faith is dormant.

One day at a time

Matthew 6:34

—Each day has enough trouble of its own.

If I live one day at a time, I stay in the present and my day goes by without projecting that bad things will happen in the future. I experience trouble every day it comes in all sorts of ways. Worrying about the things that everyone worries about will drive you mad. If I want a day filled with joy, pray to God for a good day.

Focusing on the present is exactly what I need to do, but I forget to do it. So I need to remember that one day at a time is what God calls for me to practice and live, and is found in the Our Father Prayer. Try to think about only what can be done for the day instead of what has to be done for the rest of your life.

Renovation

Romans 8:28

For those God foreknew he also predestined to be conformed to the likeness of his Son—.

When you renovate your house or car, you change the appearance of the house or car. When God renovates your heart your life shows His love. Also, your life reflects Jesus. Sometimes the change is painful to under go, and it hurts when your in it. But God's renovation is all for God's will.

Whatever the things are that God chooses to do in your life, it molds you to the likeness of his Son Jesus. Being like Jesus you will show fruits of the Spirit.

Transformation will be a life long process that will change the appearance of your life to others around you. If anyone asks you why or you what happened to you? Tell them that you now have a personal relationship with Jesus.

Repentance

Luke 13:3

I tell you, no! but unless you repent you too will perish.

    Repentance is necessary to come to salvation. God wants everyone to come to repentance and come to salvation. If you tell him the sins you have committed before his eyes it is a promise that He will forgive you.

    Believers that are children of God will need to clean house if they are sinning. By confessing your wrongs you will have a right relation with God and able to do his will. It is also a promise that you will receive the Holy Spirit if you repent. If you are not a believer yet, repent and believe in Jesus and God will accept you as his children. Being a child of God you will go to heaven instead of perishing.

Prospering in life

Jeremiah 29:11

"For I know the plans I have for you," Declares the Lord, "plans to prosper you and not to harm you, plans to give you hope and a future."

    Sometimes we think, when am I going to get what I want? That's not for us to decide. Sometimes God gives us what we want when we want it and sometime we never get what we want. Eternity though will be the greatest thing we ever get.

    I have been given hope and it never dies out. A future with everything I could need lies ahead. If you don't have hope for your future know that God has it under control. He will be able to direct your life which ever way he decides to. God has the strings of course of your life in his hands. Although he allows us to do things he disapproves of he still watches us and makes opportunities arise in our lives. God's plan is for the best and will reunite us with our relatives who have passed on.

The happy ending

Job 42:12

The Lord blessed the latter part of Job's life more than the first.

Job suffered great loss and was in much pain because of it. He lost his children due to fires and attacks. His body was covered with sores. He lost all of his animals which back then provided food, clothing, and transportation. Even though God allowed such bad adversity into Job's life he was a winner. Job and his friends reasoned like us why do things like this happen. Also, Job asks for someone to talk to intermediate between him and God. Job wanted answers about his circumstances. When he finally got through his problems and then the Lord blessed him. He was blessed so much that he had double everything he had lost. This is not for everyone though; the Lord can bless who ever he chooses to.

Heart's Desire

Psalm 37:4

Delight yourself in the Lord and he will give you the desires of your heart.

Devoting your life to God will yield the best things you could wish for. The Lord gives you what you desire when you take time for him. Who wouldn't reciprocate back something for true love and devotion? I know that I like to help those who help me.

For example I so desired to have a new truck and the work came in so that I made enough money to buy one. Before this happened, I was going to church, singing songs of praise, tithing money, and praying on a daily basis. God was honored by my love and made available the work in the textile industry. When the work dried up, I felt like I did something wrong. Maybe this closed avenue would make room for a bigger opportunity that would someday happen.

Turn your burden to God

Psalm 55:22

Cast your cares on the Lord and he will sustain you; he will never let the righteous fall.

    I like to hold on to my problems and solve them myself. I have real victory when God solves them for me. Trying to work out everything for my own ends is tiring. If I am working against God the problem may never be solved. When God carries your cares he can sustain them because he is greater that we are. I can spend all my energy trying to solve my problems and never get anywhere. If we are God's children he will take care of us and our worries. This verse shows this and is a help for knowing where you can send your worries to.

Angel's care

Psalm 91:11

For he will command his angels concerning you to guard you in all your ways;

Knowing that God has his angels watching and guarding me in all circumstances is comforting.

I once backed up my truck and it stopped suddenly, right behind me was a telephone pole. You could say that an angel blocked my truck from hitting the pole. I don't know if you believe in angels, but when this happened to me I did. I knew something was watching over me that instant. Things like that don't happen every day but it is cool when they do. My truck could have crashed into the pole and knocked that beam on top of my truck. God have must have needed me for something to protect me like that.

God the Judge

Psalm 96:13

He will judge the world in righteousness and the peoples in his truth.

    When I think of God as a judge my mind is struck with fear. Even though my sins are taken away by Jesus on the cross, I feel inadequate for salvation at times. Other times though my faith is swelling and I know my Lord has forgiven me. My righteousness is not always the best it could be. At this point I need to read the Word or the Bible and focus on God's revealed truths. When I do God reveals to me things I could improve on or wisdom that I don't know of yet.

    God's truth is the Bible and when you read the Bible, it fills you with God's truths. Knowing that the Cross was sufficient for God's payment of sin makes our faith real and strong. So we don't need to fear God the Judge.

Healing of the Nations

Revelation 22:2

And the leaves of the tree are for the healing of the nations.

In heaven there is a river which flows down the middle of the street and on each side of it are trees. These trees yield fruit and leaves. God has said that these leaves are for the healing of the nations.

Our nations are countries as you may call them, and are always having wars and hatred against each other. Look at what happen to the Jews in World War II, and look at what happened to the blacks in the pre Civil War. Both of these wars were wrong and caused racism. The leaves I believe are to heal our hatreds against other races and let us live at peace with each other for eternity. This would make all races get along and love each other.

God's eternal Love

Psalm 136:26

Give thanks to the God of heaven.
His love endures forever.

    Everyday I forget about people but the Lord doesn't. The lord cares about everyone. This can be seen by the rain. If, it didn't rain the fields wouldn't grow their crops and we would not have any food to eat. All the earth depends on food, because of this the Lord waters the fields with rain. This is a demonstration of his love.

    We should give thanks to God for this. I believe when we acknowledge him, we remember that we are under his presence and love. God made us for a reason, this I think is so we he know all about him. His holy nature is one aspect of his character that I had to find out about through reading the Bible and going to church.

Meditating on the word

Matthew 4:4

Jesus answered "It is written: Man does not live on bread alone but on every word that comes from the mouth of God."

Being a child of God you will need to meditate on word of God and live on it. It will show you God's will and his law. This will encourage, strengthen, and give you hope. It will encourage you to live a holy life. It will strengthen your faith. It will give hope for the future.

How can you obey the law without knowing it? Keeping your mind fresh in his words and commands makes you walk a righteous life.

When you walk in the path of righteousness, it is by the Holy Spirit who dwells within you.

Trials

James 1:12

Blessed is the man who perseveres under trial, because when he has stood the test, he will receive the crown of life that God has promised to those who love him.

I once had a problem with the heat in my apartment and I thought it would never be right. This was a trial that I didn't take with grace. I was so angry that I almost became of no use to myself. This problem was frustrating enough to make me yell at the ones I love.

My confidence in God to solve this problem was small. This just seemed to aggravate me.

The man who perseveres under trail will build his faith strong, and upon it will save his soul. We face many trails in life and there's always another one around the bend. So we need to have thee endurance of a marathon runner.

Rapture

Corinthians 15:51-52

Listen, I tell you a mystery: We will not all
sleep, but we will all be changed—
In a flash, in the twinkling of an eye, at the
last trumpet. For the trumpet will sound, the
dead will be raised imperishable, and we
will be changed.

    The prophecy of the rapture some day

will be fulfilled. At this time, believers

will meet Christ in the air and have a

new spiritual body and live with Christ

forever. Those that have died will be there

too, and they will receive a new body

also. This event could happen at any time

because Jesus said I am coming soon.

    So we should walk obedient and holy

lives. That would make the Lord happy.

Just think you may meet the Lord in

the air any day now. This can give you

strength to get through the day. If you are

in pain or suffering, hold on because Jesus

is coming for you.

The Son of God

Romans 1:4

And who through the Spirit of holiness was declared with power to be the Son of God by his resurrection from the dead: Jesus Christ our Lord.

Jesus was in heaven before he came to earth. Jesus was born into this world though the virgin Mary and conceived by the Holy Spirit. Jesus existed since the beginning of time and now sits at the right hand of the Father.

When Jesus asked Peter who he thought he was, Peter answered, Matthew 16:16 "you are the Christ, the Son of the living God." Jesus said he had authority to lay down his body and authority take it up from the dead. Jesus said he would destroy the temple and would raise it up in three days, and Jesus did so. His resurrection from the dead shows the Power of God and establishes that he is the Son of God.

Faithfulness

Proverbs 3:3

Let love and faithfulness never leave you; bind them around your neck, write them on the tablet of your heart.

In the Book of Proverbs this chapter says you will win favor in the sight of God and Man if you never let love and faithfulness leave you. I found this to be true. People respect it when you say you are going to be some where and you are. If you are not some where you are supposed to be people lose trust in you. I like to try to keep all my appointments.

Also I try to love my friends, God, and family as much as I can. The sinful nature breaks my relationships apart and causes a disconnection of love. God's favor will be given to those who love him through obedience and they will be blessed. The same is somewhat true about your friends if they are genuine.

Gossip

James 3:6

The tongue also is a fire, a world of evil among the parts of the body. It corrupts the whole person,

    If you have never said anything behind someone else's back you're perfect. But like most of us we have. Some people long to here some juicy info on another person. This is the way bad rumors get started. Only tell others things you would say if that person were there and in front of you. The tongue is filled with evil and lashes out hurtful things against other people when you are mad. I try to tell people I don't gossip and if that doesn't work I stay away from the people who like to gossip.

    You don't like it when others tell bad things about you right? So don't make up lies about other people who you are mad at.

Golden Jerusalem

Revelation 21:18

The wall was made of pure jasper, and the city of pure gold, as pure as glass.

God has made the city beautiful as a bride dressed for her husband. Our new heavenly home will be built by God and not by us. People build our homes here on earth. Why is God building us a city? I think it is because we will need a place to live and to worship the Lord. Possible the city will have rooms for the rewards a believer gets upon his or her judgment of works.

We are not saved by works but we will receive rewards for our actions here on earth. Are souls are saved by our faith in Jesus. We are not under the wrath of God if we believe in Jesus.

God's Commandments

Psalm 119:59

I have considered my ways and have turned my steps to your statutes.

    When God's commandments are broken by me, I have to be forgiven by God and not by me. God forgives them after I confess them to him. So the commandments are Gods and they need to be forgiven by God.

    After I repent of my sin, the guilt I have will lift and my heart will be in right before God Almighty. When I turn to Gods statutes I can live a righteous life and be blessed by God with blessings that unfold into my life everyday.

Abiding in the vine

John 15:5

I am the vine; you are the branches. If a man remains in me and I in him, he will bear much fruit; apart from me you can do nothing.

When a grape grows on a vine, the vine supplies the food and water and energy for the grape to grow. We are like that grape. Our food or help comes from Jesus. He says that apart from him you can do nothing. Just like that grape if it is plucked off the vine it ceases to grow. If we can do nothing apart from him, we need him. The grape needs the vine. If we want to bear fruit, we must remain in the vine or as you may say remain in Jesus. I know that with the right circumstances the grape grows beautifully and so do we.

Bearing fruit

John 15:8

This is my Father's glory, that you bear much fruit, showing yourselves to be my disciples.

If you show the love of Christ people will be drawn toward the Lord because they will see something that the world doesn't give. Then you will bear much fruit. The fruit here that the Lord is talking about is the salvation of souls or people. Telling others about Christ will be useless if they see that you are the same as them. But if that person sees you as someone who has something that is wonderful that person will want to know why. Then you can tell them it is because of Jesus Christ. When they here this tell them in plain words why it is that you were drawn to Christ. If they here something they can relate to, they will want a relationship with Christ also. People without Christ have voids within themselves and will be filled when they repent to God.

Pruning us back

John 15:2

He cuts off every branch in me the bears no fruit he prunes so that it will be even more fruitful.

Having god the Father as our gardener we will grow like a sunflower. As a sunflower we will plant a lot of seeds if we are pruned back. God prunes us back by his ways. When we are useful to God we can plant lots of seeds and maybe some seeds will take root and develop into Christians. Our seed falls on all types of ground. God works out our best characteristics and makes them for his purposes he chooses. What ever faults we have are cut back. As this happens we grow in the way he desires. Dying to oneself causes more usefulness to God. This is because we care more about his things than ourselves.

You're invited

Revelation 3:20

Here I am! I stand at the door and knock. If anyone hears my voice and opens the door, I will come in and eat with him and he with me.

Jesus invites us to him through the message of the Gospel. If we accept his invitation, we are invited to spend eternity with him. He knocks on your heart and asks to come in. If you accept his invitation, he enters into you.

When you remain quite, you can hear well. At these times the Lord sometimes speaks to us so that we can know him. Letting the Lord into our lives will change us and our destiny. If you pray for him to reveal himself to you he will. God can show you things that will draw your heart in. It's amazing the stories I have heard about the ways people have come to know the Lord. All the stories are different but they are all good.

Gates of heaven

Psalm 118:19

Open for me the gates of righteousness
I will enter and give thanks to the Lord.

    This Psalm gives an idea of how great it will be to be in the Lords presence. We most assuredly will thank the Lord for his great mercy. Thinking of the gates of righteousness I imagine something out of a movie like where God and his angels are awaiting our arrival. Of course I don't want to die yet, but knowing that I meet him gives me a sense of purpose. This comes to me because I have had numerous difficulties in life such as an appendix operation, hit in the head with an aluminum, baseball bat, and different health problems.

    To many times I think that this life is meant to drive us crazy, but really I find that everything is for a purpose. What the purpose is at the time I don't know, but when I look back I see it.

Instruction

Proverbs 16:20

Whoever gives heed to instruction prospers, and blessed is he who trusts in the Lord.

When someone tells me something to do at first I think don't do it, but then I do it. Why do I always at first don't want to do it? This is my rebellious spirit I have. When you're submissive you can gain a great deal from taking an instruction. Why is it that the person who we get it from is never the one we want to hear it from? If I take the instructions, as long as they are right and not improper, I will show benefits of listening.

I once listened to a friend of mine for where to buy tires because I used to get them at the junk yard. The new tires worked good and didn't blow out all the time. It did of course cost more money, but the investment was worth while.

Having no Fear because God is on your side

Psalm 27:1

The Lord is my light and my salvation—whom shall I fear?

    The Lord is our salvation and gives us assurance to fear nothing. This is because our salvation anchors us to his presence. With this you can be confident before people with God behind you. Why fear man, if God has everything in his hands and is sovereign? Does not God determine what happens to us? If so, no one can do anything to you that would make you lose out on your salvation. All the ends of things are determined by God's control. Let him be the director of your life. This will bring you comfort and remove all your fears.

God is good

Psalm 135:3

Praise the Lord, for the Lord is good;

    I know some people think that God is just all about lighting bolts and thunder, but the Lord is good. He wants good things for us and doesn't do evil. He permits evil in the world, but by no means does evil. When September 11 happened, people asked why God? Things like this we may never know but God knows. People always want an answer for everything, but that is a mistake because not everything is for us to know. When we take trust in God it is by faith not by sight. You may say we are kind of blind to certain things that are in front of us. This is why I try not to think about why but wonder about he is good. He if he were not good, your birth may never have even occurred.

God works things for our good

Romans 8:28

And we know that all things work together for good to those who love God

Seeing the good in all things is hard, but when we put this scripture to work we find that all things are for our good. Most things don't feel that way but God brings good out of the worst things in your lives. For instance I got caught speeding in my car, but at the speed I was going could have killed myself and my friend. When I lost my license, I was angry. I did drive safer in the end. If you look back you can see things that brought good things to past out of your hurt. Of course we don't know what's ahead in life but with God as the taxi driver all we need to do is sit back and enjoy the ride.

Trusting in your self

Proverbs 28:26

He who trusts in himself is a fool,
But he who walks in wisdom is kept safe.

Trusting in your self is something I do to frequently. I should be trusting in the Lord. But what am I doing relying on my self for every thing? I need to step back and relax. Remember that God is control of everything and it is futile for me to try to trust in anything but him.

If I think I have everything under my control, I am in for a disaster. When I let God run my life I am certain that those things will work out. It's like Murphy's Law which states if anything can go wrong it will. My life goes smoothly when God is running my life.

Finding a home

John 14:23

Jesus replied, "If anyone loves me, he will obey my teaching. My father will love him, and we will come to him and make our home with him.

Jesus says that we will live with him if we obey his teaching. Spending life after death must be amazing, because we will be in heaven. Just think that after you die there's another home waiting for you on the other side. This is where you will spend eternity. Jesus paid the price for eternal life on the cross. No matter how many good things you do that's not enough to pay the price. He died for the wrongs you have done in the eyes of God. By believing in him and trusting him as savior all your sin will be covered by his blood.

Sin Vs. Sins

Romans 7:20

Now if I do what I do not want to do, it is no longer I who do it, but it is sin living in me that does it.

When we sin, we sin because we have sin in us. The difference between sin and sins is that with sins are the one you do. And sin is the nature of sin that dwells within us. Thought sin has been crucified by the cross and us also. Therefore we should not let sin rule us, but live holy lives.

I have done lots on sins but sin is why I do it. The sin came from when Adam fell in the Garden of Eden. People should confess their sins and they will be forgiven. Our nature can change if you are in Christ and should. When we stay in our old ways we are not remembering that we crucified sin we were baptized.

Jesus does Miracles

John 9:21

But how he can see know, who opened his eyes, we don't know.

The Pharisees couldn't believe that Jesus healed this man from being blind. This miracle was just one of the thousand that Jesus did when he was on earth. Jesus healed people to show he could forgive sin and that he was the Christ.

People that saw these miracles became followers of him and at one point he had five thousand following him. Here he feed all of them and they were happy. When Jesus told his disciples that they would need to give up their lives to follow him many left his side. But the twelve stayed and proclaimed that Gospel.

Jesus eats with the tax Collector

Matthew 9:10

While Jesus was having dinner at Matthew's house, many tax collectors and "sinners" came and ate with him and his disciples.

    Jesus eat with Matthew the tax collector. This was seen as a way out thing back then because tax collectors where thought of as bad people. Jesus extended his love to these people and they received him. Jesus showed that no matter what you did for a living that person could become a follower of his.

    Matthew became a disciple and followed Jesus around the world back then. Tax collectors are only doing their jobs and Jesus showed that they too are good people. Having dinner with the tax collectors must have been interesting because tax collectors are thought of as greedy people and Jesus preached giving to poor, not taking from the poor.

Jesus pays his tax

Matthew 17:27

—Take it and give it to them for my tax and yours.

Here in this Gospel of Matthew, we find that Jesus paid his tax to the temple. We should likewise pay our taxes when they are due. Its not easy no do the right thing, but we can follow the example that was left us by Jesus. Paying the government what we think we should makes us cringe. I know that doing everything where I live is complex. The only why to get everything done is not think about it because if you do you will be overwhelmed. The more and more complex the world becomes the more responsibility people tend to have. The thing that makes paying our taxes easier is letting someone else do it for you.

Trusting in the Lord

Proverbs 3:5

Trust in the Lord with all your heart
And lean not on your own understanding;

    When I trust in the lord I have peace. When I trust in myself I have negative projection and worry. Though in life it is necessary to take action when you have a problem, I find letting God care about it gives me peace. Prayer helps turn it over into the hands of God.

    People ask me "What am I going to do about it?" The next thing that happens is I lean on my own understanding instead of trusting that God will work it out for me. I could worry forever, but that wouldn't achieve anything good.

    God solved the problem of salvation and if you trust in him he will bring you home to heaven. If you trust in him you will never be put to shame.

Crucifixation Prophecy

Isaiah chapter 53

Jesus prophecy is in the Bible you can read all about what is going to happen to him on the cross. This prophecy tells that Jesus will be nailed and no bone broken. In the New Testament we see that this happens to Jesus. His death was for us and was a great show of love and sacrifice for us.

Drunkenness

Ephesians 5:18

Do not get drunk on wine, which leads to debauchery. Instead be filled with the Spirit.

If you like to get drunk, you're sinning against God. Here in Ephesians we are told to put away with drunkenness and instead be filled with the Spirit.

The sin of drunkenness is one that after you're in it, it's hard to get out of. Like it is written sin gives birth to sin and when sin is full grown it brings death. Many of my friends in life have died due to this sin. The whole life style is one of rebellion against God. People trapped into this sin focus on the effects of bottle and worship it. Therefore they block out the Spirit and become useless to themselves and other.

Though, I know many, who have recovered from this sin. Ask God to forgive you and choose life instead of the drink.

Jesus betrayal

John 11:57

But the chief priests and Pharisees had given orders that if anyone found out where Jesus was, he should report it so that they might arrest him.

Just like the way the priests and Pharisees were jealous of Jesus, we too are sometimes jealous of others. I know some people who are just like the Pharisees and think of murdering the one they are jealous of. For Jesus it was his mission, he was to be betrayed into the hands of evil men and be crucified. This great injustice God turned into the greatest triumph of all time. Also, God made good out of evil, which is called divine providence.

When we hold an evil though or covet something another person has we are jealous. This jealousy could cause harm to ourselves and is a sin that God doesn't approve of. Live holy lives and be content with little.

God's Power

John 11:25 KJV

Jesus said unto her, I am the resurrection, and the life; he that believeth in me, though he were dead, yet shall he live:

When I think that God has the power to raise our bodies from the dead, I'm amazed. This is something I can't do and neither can you. This power rests only in God. Jesus is the resurrection and the life with this being he holds the keys to life and death.

There's a movie out Bruce Almighty and the actor has the power of God. God's power even in this comedy can be seen as dramatic and awesome. I guess people would like to have power over different things in life, but only God does. God can make something happen, if he chooses to let it occur.

But if you believe in Jesus, he says you will live after death.

Asking for a big thing

Mark 11:23-24

And Jesus answering saith unto tem, Have Faith in God. For Verily I say unto you, That whosoever shall say unto this mountain, Be thou removed, and be thou cast into the sea; and shall not doubt in his heart, but shall believe that those things which he saith come to pass; he shall have whatsoever he saith.

Wow just think, God could answer a big prayer like that, but Jesus says you need to believe in your heart that it has already come to pass. Having faith in God to move your mountain what ever it be, could be difficult because sometimes we forget what. God is capable of.

Plus, if God has just done something great in your life you may have more faith than before. Psalm 78 tells about Moses' answered prayers. Read about prayers answered by God in the Holy Bible.

God's Provision and Love

Romans 5:8 KJV

But God commendeth his love toward us, in that while we were yet sinners, Christ died for us.

Jesus choosing to give his life for me is amazing. Jesus loves me enough to die for me. Jesus' mission was the cross. His cross and his shed blood on it wipes away all my sin. Every time I worry about my sin I just have to bring it to the cross and remember Jesus death was its payment. God accepts his sacrifice for the sins of the whole world.

Everyone needs to come to repentance for eternal life. God's love provided a way and that is through his Son, Jesus. Jesus loves us enough to endure a cross of death. Think of all the pain and heart ache that was taken for us to be accepted as children of God.

Who should judge?

Matthew 7:1

Do not judge and you will not be judged.

Many times, the way someone talks or dresses make us take an opinion of them. Possible we judge them and want to feel superior to them.

Maybe, we base our judgment on the fact that they are not saved and that judgment is for God alone. We should not play God or judge others because we ourselves are not in right in doing so.

I have judged others not knowing the evil that was stored up in my heart. You only need to worry about your own sin and repent from it, and do not worry about someone else's sin and judge them because of it.

Meditating on the word

Matthew 4:4

Jesus answered "It is written: Man does not live on bread alone but on every word that comes from the mouth of God."

Being a child of God you will need to meditate on word of God and live on it. It will show you God's will and his law. This will encourage, strengthen, and give you hope. It will encourage you to live a holy life. It will strengthen your faith. It will give hope for the future.

How can you obey the law without knowing it? Keeping your mind fresh in his commands makes you walk a righteous life.

When you walk in the path of righteousness, it is by the Holy Spirit who dwells within you.

Trials

James 1:12

Blessed is the man who perseveres under trial, because when he has stood the test, he will receive the crown of life that God has promised to those who love him.

I once had a problem with the heat in my apartment and I thought it would never be right. This was a trial that I didn't take with grace. I was so angry that I almost became of no use to myself. This problem was frustrating enough to make me yell at the ones I love.

My confidence in God to solve this problem was small. This just seemed to aggravate me.

The man who perseveres under trail will build his faith strong, and upon it will save his soul. We face many trails in life and there's always another one around the bend. So we need to have thee endurance of a marathon runner.

Rapture

Corinthians 15:51-52

Listen, I tell you a mystery: We will not all sleep, but we will all be changed—
In a flash, in the twinkling of an eye, at the last trumpet. For the trumpet will sound, the dead will be raised imperishable, and we will be changed.

    The prophecy of the rapture some day will be fulfilled. At this time, believers will meet Christ in the air and have a new spiritual body and live with Christ forever. Those that have died will be there too, and they will receive a new body also. This event could happen at any time because Jesus said I am coming soon.

    So we should walk obedient and holy lives. That would make the Lord happy. Just think you may meet the Lord in the air any day now. This can give you strength to get through the day. If you are in pain or suffering, hold on because Jesus is coming for you.

The Son of God

Romans 1:4

And who through the Spirit of holiness was declared with power to be the Son of God by his resurrection from the dead: Jesus Christ our Lord.

Jesus was in heaven before he came to earth. Jesus was born into this world though the virgin Mary and conceived by the Holy Spirit. Jesus existed since the beginning of time and now sits at the right hand of the Father.

When Jesus asked Peter who he thought he was, Peter answered, Matthew 16:16 "you are the Christ, the Son of the living God." Jesus said he had authority to lay down his body and authority take it up from the dead. Jesus said he would destroy the temple and would raise it up in three days, and Jesus did so. His resurrection from the dead shows the Power of God and establishes that he is the Son of God.

Faithfulness

Proverbs 3:3

Let love and faithfulness never leave you; bind them around your neck, write them on the tablet of your heart.

In the Book of Proverbs this chapter says you will win favor in the sight of God and Man if you never let love and faithfulness leave you. I found this to be true. People respect it when you say you are going to be some where and you are. If you are not some where you are supposed to be people lose trust in you. I like to try to keep all my appointments.

Also I try to love my friends, God, and family as much as I can. The sinful nature breaks my relationships apart and causes a disconnection of love. God's favor will be given to those who love him through obedience and they will be blessed. The same is somewhat true about your friends if they are genuine.

Trusting in the Lord

Proverbs 3:5

Trust in the Lord with all your heart
And lean not on your own understanding;

When I trust in the lord I have peace. When I trust in myself I have negative projection and worry. Though in life it is necessary to take action when you have a problem, I find letting God care about it gives me peace. Prayer helps turn it over into the hands of God.

People ask me "What am I going to do about it?" The next thing that happens is I lean on my own understanding instead of trusting that God will work it out for me. I could worry forever, but that wouldn't achieve anything good.

God solved the problem of salvation and if you trust in him he will bring you home to heaven. If you trust in him you will never be put to shame.

Golden Jerusalem

Revelation 21:18

The wall was made of pure jasper, and the city of pure gold, as pure as glass.

God has made the city beautiful as a bride dressed for her husband. Our new heavenly home will be built by God and not by us. People build our homes here on earth. Why is God building us a city? I think it is because we will need a place to live and to worship the Lord. Possible the city will have rooms for the rewards a believer gets upon his or her judgment of works.

We are not saved by works but we will receive rewards for our actions here on earth. Are souls are saved by our faith in Jesus. We are not under the wrath of God if we believe in Jesus.

BVG